THE COMPLET BASTARD'S GUIDE TO GOLF

by Jed Pascoe

First Published in Great Britain by
Powerfresh Limited
3 Gray Street
Northampton
England
NN1 3QQ

Telephone 0604 30996 Country Code 44
Facsimile 0604 21013

© January 1993 Jed Pascoe

THE COMPLETE BASTARD'S GUIDE TO GOLF
ISBN 1 874125 16 3

Printed in Britain by Avalon Print Ltd., Northampton.

INTRODUCTION

BY ROSIE AND RENNIE

"GOLF... THE GAME OF LORDS AND PEASANTS ALIKE"

"INVENTED BY THE SCOTS, WASN'T IT?"

"THERE'S A BUNCH OF BASTARDS FOR YOU.."

"YER.. REMEMBER ANGUS 'THE AXE' MCSWEENEY?"

"A CLASS ACT AND NO MISTAKE!"

"HE ALWAYS TOOK MORE STROKES THAN NECESSARY..."

"HACK HACK HACK..."

"SO HERE'S A BOOK ABOUT HOW TO WIN AT GOLF...."

SELECTING THE CORRECT EQUIPMENT..

IRON MAIDEN →

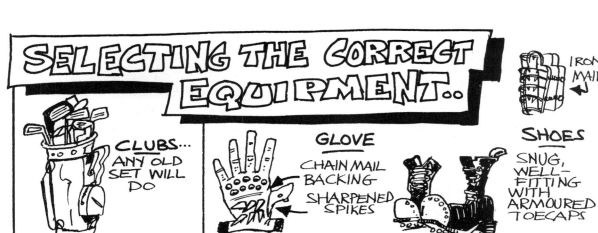

CLUBS... ANY OLD SET WILL DO

GLOVE
CHAIN MAIL BACKING
SHARPENED SPIKES

SHOES
SNUG, WELL-FITTING WITH ARMOURED TOECAPS

THUMBSCREW

BALL MARKER
FOR MARKING OPPONENTS BALLS

SILLY HAT →

MANNLICHER 75MM...
RECOMMENDED BY PROFESSIONALS FOR THOSE AWKWARD SHOTS

RIP

MARKER PEGS

FURTHER EQUIPMENT TIPS ON FOLLOWING PAGES

BEFORE COMMENCING PLAY, INFORM YOUR OPPONENT YOU HAD A BAD DAY YESTERDAY...

ONLY SHOT FOUR UNDER PAR

CLOTHING

NOT RECOMMENDED

- SAM TORRANCE HAT
- JACK NICKLAUS SHIRT
- SEVE BALLESTEROS JUMPER
- PAYNE STEWART PLUS TWO'S
- TONY JACKLIN CLUBS
- LEE TREVINO SOCKS
- TOMMY HORTON SHOES

MEANS SOD ALL

MIDDLE CHOICE

- GOOD QUALITY POLAROID SUNGLASSES
- DARK, SOMBRE COAT
- UZI 9MM MACHINE PISTOL

MEANS BUSINESS

HIGHLY RECOMMENDED

- UVEX TANK GOGGLES
- FULL NATO BATTLE DRESS (N. EUROPE CAMO PATTERN)
- SMITH & AND WESSON SURVIVAL KNIFE
- AK47 ASSAULT RIFLE WITH PARATROOPER STOCK

MEANS WE ARE PLAYING TO WIN

..... I DID WARN YOU TO WATCH OUT FOR THE TRAP ON THE NINTH.....!

DEMONSTRATING THE CORRECT USE OF SEVEN IRONS

THE SHOT OFF THE GREEN

EFFECT:
YOUR OPPONENT MAKES A PERFECT SHOT ONTO THE GREEN — THEN HIS BALL MYSTERIOUSLY ROLLS OUT-OF-BOUNDS!

HOW THE TRICK IS DONE:
BEFORE COMMENCING PLAY, YOU INJECT A LARGE AMOUNT OF IRON FILINGS INTO YOUR OPPONENT'S BALL.

THEN YOUR ASSOCIATE COMPLETES THE OPERATION WITH A LARGE MAGNET!

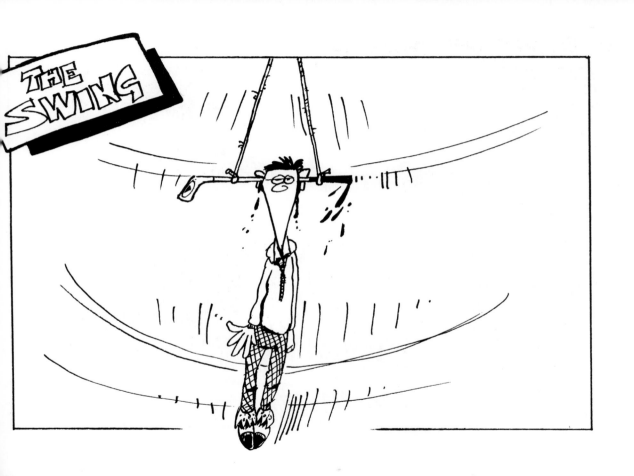

TIQUETTE
A GOOD GOLFER ALWAYS REPLACES HIS DIVOTS ...
DDBLATT! DDBLATT! DDDBLATT!

The Immovable Ball

The Effect:
Your opponent goes to hit a ball in an easy lie— but it won't budge!

WELL STUCK!

How the Trick is Done:
While your opponent's back is turned, you drive a 24" steel stake through his ball into the ground

BALL
GROUND LEVEL
←STAKE

OOH .... MR. PETERSON — I MUCH PREFER
STROKEPLAY TO MATCHPLAY.--

NOW THEN— WHAT WAS ALL THAT
NONSENSE ABOUT BLACK BALLS?

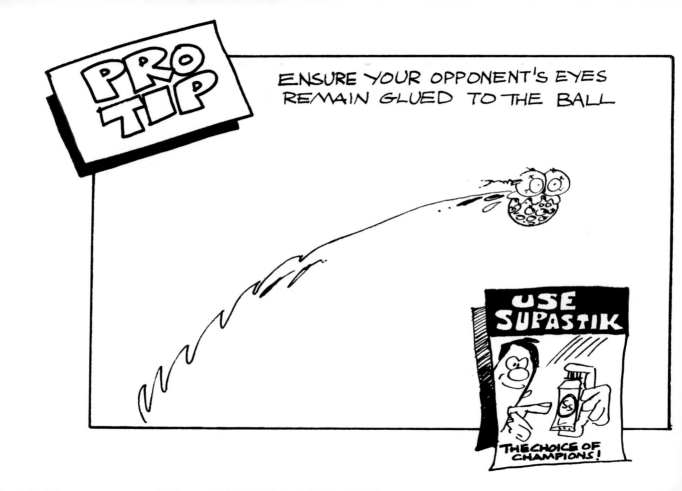

SELECTING EXACTLY THE RIGHT CLUB EVERY TIME

EFFECT: YOU ARE A BRILLIANT JUDGE OF DISTANCE

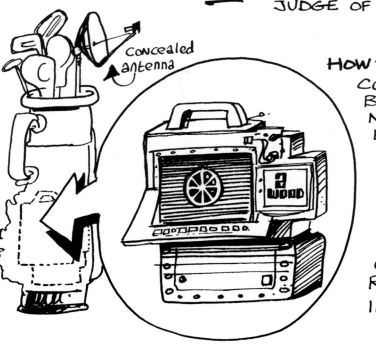

Concealed antenna

2 WOOD

HOW THE TRICK IS DONE:

CONCEALED IN YOUR BAG IS AN ISRAELI NAVAL PATTERN EARLY WARNING SYSTEM, ADAPTED FOR USE ON THE FAIRWAY... A GLANCE AT THE DIGITAL READOUT GIVES YOU THE RIGHT CLUB IN SECONDS!

YET ANOTHER HOARY OLD BUNKER GAG...

JED PASCOE
NATIONAL AND INTERNATIONAL
AWARD WINNING
CARTOONIST.
LIVING PROOF THAT
EMPTY VESSELS MAKE
MOST NOISE..
TOTALLY CONFUSED BY
LIFE, HE LIVES MAINLY
IN HIS BELEAGURED
IMAGINATION - WHICH
IS ENOUGH TO
CONFUSE ANYONE. AND
STILL LOOKING FOR FAME
AND FORTUNE, IF ANYONE
OUT THERE IS INTERESTED.